¡VIVA LA VITA!

Chris Felver
1990
San Francisco

THE
POET
EXPOSED

THE
POET
EXPOSED

Portraits by Christopher Felver

Prologue by Gary Snyder
Foreword by Robert Creeley
Afterword by William E. Parker

ALFRED VAN DER MARCK EDITIONS · NEW YORK

Editorial director: Robert Walter

Managing editor: Leonard Neufeld

Designer: John Brogna

Cover design: Jon Farhat

Photographic printing: Professional Photographic
Services, Eddie Dyba/Timothy Burman,
San Francisco

Excerpt from R. M. Rilke's *Letters to a Young Poet* (trans. by
M.D. Herter Norton) used with permission of W. W. Norton & Co.

Library of Congress Cataloging-in-Publication Data

Felver, Christopher, 1946–
   The poet exposed.

   Includes index.
   1. Poets, American—20th century—Portraits.
2. Poets, American—20th century—Autographs.
3. American poetry—20th century—Manuscripts—
Facsimiles. 4. Manuscripts, American—Facsimiles.
5. Photography—Portraits.   I. Title.
PS129.F45   1986   811'.5'09   [B]   85-40824
ISBN 0-912383-22-4
ISBN 0-912383-23-2 (pbk.)

Printed in Italy by Poligrafiche Bolis, Bergamo.

First printing: June 1986

IN MEMORY OF TED BERRIGAN

"Tho I grew tall, &
huge of frame, I
had a perfect heart."
— Ted Berrigan
July 26,
1982

PROLOGUE

the hand and face of the
poet -- birdtracks, wrinkles,
leaves blown in dust, it's
good to see hand and face
brought together here by
Chris Felver. Neither
can lie, calligraphy is
character, and we measure
each other "at the crossroads
of the new world" by the
look in the eye. Chris
draws both out with his gentle,
insistent skill--no escape.

Gary Snyder
29 November '83

FOREWORD

How hard it seems, finally, to see another, to
apprehend who it is *is* there, and how constantly
fragile the whole exchange, even at best. I had been
thinking of Robert Burns' wry emphasis, "to see
ourselves as others see us..." But that's not the
point here. Nor is Eliot's: "To prepare a face to
meet the faces that you meet..."

> There will be time to murder and create,
> And time for all the works and days of hands
> That lift and drop a question on your plate...

To define a quick context—faces are *appearances*,
the visage, the countenance, the expression of the
countenance, the outward aspect, the determined
dignity, self-respect, what's manifest as *face value*.
Face has a function involved with making (*facere*)
as *make-up* would testify. It looks like.

To make a portrait of that subtle, manip-
ulative occasion is complexly demanding. I'm
struck that *portrait* has a root sense of "to draw
forth," which in turn provokes a sense of "draw"
I'd never before thought of. The painter Kitaj called
the act of drawing another human being the sum
and measure of the art. It is an entirely human one
in all respects. No other relation can so define
imagination or the power of seeing literally. Photography proves a consummate instance.

The old-time portraiture, like that of Bach-
rach, in the northeast, had the clear purpose of
social investment. My Uncle Hap worked for their
company in the thirties and contrived to have
portraits done of his mother and father. Their faces
are backed by some curious indeterminancy of lit
cloud or smoke; they look solidly secure, bemus-
edly accommodating—and are in no way my
grandparents. There is certainly nothing wrong

with that fact. There are other values at work, and image serves by its contrivance to hoist these two commoners into the apparent ranks of the financially blest. We might have some questions, and I don't know what they thought of it all. (The same uncle had battered together an extremely tentative "family tree," which gave us remarkable affiliations — again all bankrupt, in fact.) We did see someone, however, of our relation, in a place we had heard about but never known, and that gave some added dimension to our otherwise mundane lives. Yet the ploy is the same as the undertaker's exceptional use of rouge, the suit bought just for that final occasion, the hair curled at last. Such "drawing forth" as that can be has little to do with its subjects.

Chris Felver's concerns are intensely otherwise, and here one sees writers, *poets* — those most blest by an art but also made most vulnerable. There's no money in it, like they say, or at best very, very little. And so the casual interest fades. (Had any a lingering doubt concerning Cardenal, to see him so comfortable here must banish it forever.) The photographer is a friend, the faces are remarkably open, and a reflective small grin echoes from page to page. I think it is that, for the most part, all are at home in the world, and this person come to call, with his camera, is there in like manner, equally open. What drama there is is muted, faces are extremely without artifice, look for the most part straight forward. So the man looking at them is by that defined.

W. C. Williams makes clear his anger at the cost of Man Ray's portrait of him, if flattered, possibly, by the occasion. He looks alert, raw, vulnerable. Without question Man Ray has put him in his place (in contrast with the portrait by Charles Sheeler). Berenice Abbott's portraits of the same period — of Djuna Barnes or Joyce, for example — show a far more intimate sense of the person sitting there. It isn't just that she cares, but that she knows, explicitly, where she is and in what relation. She honors the subject with her clarity. Otherwise, a lot can be made of a camera, as a defensive weapon, for instance, or a means to manipulate the look — to divide and conquer, as it were. I can't think a photograph any less of a determined artifact than a painting, and to say "the camera never lies" is to be complacently ingenuous. Everything lies, with or without art, cameras included.

Therefore I much respect Felver's own integrity in this work and the commitment shown in the detail and perception his book makes evident. He has given it a significant dimension in the notes and compact poems that accompany each photograph in the person's own script. These are useful, authenticating signatures, again a substantiation of person — that someone is here, that another bears witness.

Oh haunting witness —
you've seen me again
without my knowing it.

Will my face dissolve
in my hands, will I
still remember you?

Robert Creeley
Ithaca, New York
March 9, 1986

O wind and water! Like a gale at dawn
Man hits the wave of woman She arches her throat
For the stab of his lips. Over the wallowing blood
His sudden face divides her life; his terrible gift
Wreathes her with flame!

William Everson

WILLIAM EVERSON

JACK MICHELINE

SHARON DOUBIAGO

The role of the artist
is to raise the light.

Jack Micheline

No Gods No Wars
(graffitti seen from car,
San Francisco, 4-82)

I seek the land, its Truths, its
Stories, its languages. I seek the
Lover in the land: the true unity
of the American Continents. I write
against fascism, in our thoughts,
in our languages, in our relationships:
Families, Communities, Lovers.
I write because most of the Stories
have not been written yet. I write
because we are so far from our
Selves. I write because I love.

Sharon Doubiago
Port Townsend, Washington
July 28, 1983

13

from "Days and Nights"

Z said It isn't poetry
And R said It's the greatest
    thing I ever read
And Y said I'm sick. I want to
    get up
Out of bed. Then we can talk about
    poetry
And L said There is some wine
With lunch, if you want some
And N (the bad poet) said
Listen to this. And J said I'm
    tired and
M said why don't you go to sleep,
    he laughed
And the afternoon-evening ended
At the house in bella Firenze

                    Kenneth Koch

14

KENNETH KOCH

DAVID SHAPIRO

ARAM SAROYAN

To the Earth

I fell with my father through space

Madly in love with the earth

David Shapiro

DAY AND NIGHT

Like a drop
of ink
as it hits

the water —
the whole
glass

going black:
in death
and vision,

decompression —
the soul
united

across
space and
time;

the heart
that was
blind,

a healed thing,
whole.
This

is what
the poet knows
and how he

grows apart.
Oh foolish one,
oblivious

of broken
light:
the one contained

holds the day,
the one apart
the night.

Aram Saroyan

17

This printed face doesn't see
      a curious world looking in—
Big map of nothing.

PHILIP WHALEN
SAN FRANCISCO
4 : IX : 81

PHILIP WHALEN

JOANNE KYGER

DAVID MELTZER

20

Caw Caw   Caw Caw Caw

These 3 black crows have lots of news
over burdening the other sounds
newly arrived in this location
such as myself five minutes ago ~
A definite need to be re assured
    that the present has always existed .
                    Joanne Kyger

BRINGS THE FACE OF MUSIC BACK.
ATOM BY ATOM.
                    Jim Mc Grigor

ANNE WALDMAN

Distance Traveled

> for Ted Berrigan

Hoist sail, little bark of my wit!
Mighty Captain gazing 'round —
How can I speed without you?
The light of the moon rising in Aries
makes me set a face to the hillside
Nor was our parting over
at the foot of the mountain.

Anne Waldman

NEELI CHERKOVSKI

MEI-MEI BERSSENBRUGGE

24

Like Wu Wei am I not
the self contained madman
tipping an imaginary hat
to those who pass, both
friend and stranger
and a go between
for angels and demons.

Nell: Charland

From: **Alakanak**

Everything is still moving and everything
is still one texture,
altered from sheer space to the
texture of a wall,
the route-through tightens around her
nervous system like a musculature.
It floats like a black mountain against
the night sky, although she still
remember
a mountain glimmering with ore.

Mei-mei Berssenbrugge

25

CZESLAW MILOSZ

ARMAND SCHWERNER

threads

. . . .

his heart beats like a ferryboat
between two islands, endless
dream of docking

why do you apply mathematics
to your pain
as if the turtle in a warm haze of spring
could evade its shell

the two fat inmates on the bridge
are hoping for rain
the self-confident guards
try to tell the weather apart
one and one and one and one

. . . .

his heart beats between,
an endless dream of docking
and the idea of number
does the turtle choose between itself?

Armand Schwerner

27

JIM BRODEY

RON PADGETT

For Chris Felver

the colors
are struggling
w/ the coat

      1/8/86

Jim Brodey
  XO

                        *

I was shown into the foyer
of a large mansion.

"So this is where the real Santa
claus lives." I said.

"Yes, but he's not in now,"
replied the butler.

I was shown into the foyer of a large mansion.
"So this is where the real Santa Claus lives," I said.
"Yes," replied the butler, "but he's not in now."

                                               12/24/85

Ron PADGETT

JEROME ROTHENBERG

The Nature Theater of Oklahoma

someone arrives from tishomingo

it is practically florida

it is practically the colors of summer

plen plen is the name for tea
in oklahoma

its curtains rise & fall

the shadow of a mirror
in a yellow lake

the shadow of a town called shootout

it is practically the way we are

it is practically the way the car toots
down the draw,
the car toots down the draw

Jerome Rothenberg
7/24/85

DAVID ANTIN

JACK COLLOM

32

i used to think as a poet i was
looking for the light — but theres
so much light now and its all so
bright im looking into the shadows

david ant

john moulder wins at poker

not really far
from morning & swing
into my car
& start the thing
by turning the key
& stepping on
the gas or some such
combination of
acts like the cards
fell into my red
heart
smell of smoke & the tires
hum on the rain
home

Jack Collom

CAROLYN KIZER

AFTER BASHO

Tentatively, you
slip onstage this evening,
pallid, famous moon.

— Carolyn Kizer

31 May 1985

BOB HASS

CHERI FEIN

For Chris

photographing the quick wind
in February
plum blossom, a little sun

Les
Bob Han
2-82

Intensely green, that's how the world looks
against cabbage rose wallpaper
or the room with ladies and parasols,
and somehow against this light we seem to
become more intensely ourselves.

from "32 N. Main"
Chris Fein

37

JOHN WIENERS

The Face of a Poor Woman

I have the face of a poor woman
bitter, vindictive

Though somewhat enobled
by acts of deprivation from a

man, money, clothes, house.
All these we had

but taken away by time.
Now I have only dreams and ambition
to acquire what's given at birth.
A clear day, steady gait

and mail at the post-office
plus time to account for my face.

John Wieners

39

CLARK COOLIDGE

JAMES SCHUYLER

WHEN

The knob on the radio is a ton
as I trudge up hoarse from the beach
homing on the hulks where crows and gulls
and my tongue rolls up in my head the sky
my fingers are toys too narrow for reach, then
Help Me Rhonda

Clark Coolidge

Suddenly
it's night and Tom
comes in and says,
"It's pouring buckets
out," & his blond hair
diamond-dusted with
raindrop fragments.

James Schuyler

41

LYN HEJINIAN

CHARLES BERNSTEIN

In the mass of my hallucination soaked
this international ellipsis
the sky, to speak
most intimately when speaking
of birds, is clumsy.
Ellipsis is strong, and I can't absorb it
with love
(the selfishness of continuity)
of the uncut

The Measure

The privacy of a great pain enthrones
itself on my borders and commands me
to stay at attention. Be on guard
lest the hopeless magic of unconscious
dilemmas grab hold of you in the
foggiest avenue of regret.

Charles Bernstein

ALLEN GINSBERG

R.M.D.C.

In the half light of dawn
a few birds warble
under the Pleiades.

Allen Ginsberg

for Chris Felver
July 31, 1983

PETER ORLOVSKY

JOHN GIORNO

For Chris Felver
What Luck to be The Human Bag of Plums
That Falls at Naropa Inot's School Door
Readey to Sweeten The thousand student
                                    Smile.

                        Peter Orlovsky
                        July 30, 1981
                        Boulder, Col.

UNBUILDING
A BUILDING
STONE
BY STONE,
GOING
BACKWARDS,
EVERYONE I KNOW
IS JUST LIKE ME,
THEY'RE STUPID.

John Giorno

PAUL VIOLI

DIANE DI PRIMA

"At the Corner of Muck and Myer"

for Jim Shepperd

Green light — Go.
Red light — Stop.
Yellow light — Caution.
Blinking Red light — Strong suspicions.
Blinking Blue light — Apprehension.
Yellow light with bells — Mounting fears, accusations.
White light — Sweat, speechlessness, ranting isolation.
Steady Violet light — Sunlit fragrant rooms,
　　　visitors, casual interrogations,
　　　short walks with attendant...

Paul Violi

In the west
In the east ___

This dark is the shadow
of light upon Light

Diane diPrima

Winter Solstice, 1981

CHARLES NORTH

TONY TOWLE

Three Poems

As beautiful as a jar that holds the beautiful
For centuries, or until the <u>idea</u> is full

*

Rather than its extension by mutual process
Into means, and thence the directory of endless

*

Raspberries being the perverse lachrymae
Confusing time and space. As for civic decay

Charles Wright

Chris —

Well, here I am, where
you decided I should be,
against some of the numerous
bricks of New York,
wondering if the cigarette smoke
will appear in the rectangle,
wondering how famous
the passersby think
this person really is.

Tony (Towle)
10/30/85

51

BOBBIE LOUISE HAWKINS

Why does anyone write except to speak of those things that conversation will never elicit; what is closest to the heart.... to speak of the personal with some accuracy, in the proper setting.... to have finally and for once the statement of the thing, dear thing, caught out of the void, caught onto paper; to be there at least as real as what usually happens, namely that we are so often misshapen by event, obscured by misunderstanding — I know how those papers flutter in every breeze, ephemeral. They are so fragile. Statement is fragile. It only exists later as its record — But the records of the heart return to the heart as information — And we are so hungry for it —

Bobbie Louise Hawkins

GALWAY KINNELL

JACKSON MAC LOW

Prayer

Whatever happens. Whatever
what _is_ is is what
I want. Only that. But that.

[signature]

Trope Market

In the network, in the ruin,
flashing classics gravitate,
snared, encumbered voicelessly.

Teak enticements seek, leaping
fan=shaped arras   corners
snore among in backward dispatch.

Panels glow, groan, territorialize
fetishistically in nacreous
instantaneity spookily shod.

Jackson Mac Low
4 July 1983
New York

This autograph:
7 November 1985
New York

C. K. WILLIAMS

SHARON OLDS

This is what,
at last, it is
to be
a human being.

Leaving nothing
out, not
one star, one
wren, one tear
out.

from My Parents' Wedding Night, 1937

... I leave them wrapped in that stained sheet like a
double larvum in a speckled chrysalis,
they sleep with their mouths open like teenagers,
their breath sweet, the whole room smells
delicately of champagne and semen and blood,
I let them rest, but I go back again and
                                again to that moment,
I watch them over and over until I get used to it,
like god watching Adam and Eve in the garden —
that first springing rill of dark blood,
I eye it the way the castaway stares at the
blackish life pouring out of the turtle's throat
                        where he severs it.

Sharon Olds

57

ROBERT PINSKY

LUCHA CORPI

from Poem About People

    ... The weather

Changes in the black of night,
And the dream-wind, howling across

The sopping open spaces
Of roads, golf-courses, parking lots,
Flails a commotion
In the dripping tree tops,

Tries a half-rotten shingle
Or a down-hung branch, and we
All dream it, the dark wind crossing
The wide spaces between us.

Robert Pinsky

Berkeley, 1/19/82

My father taught me to sing,
my mother to thread verses
and from my grandmother I learned
that truth can also be attained
in silence.

Tantas voces en mí ...

Lucha Corpi

As The T'ang Poet Said

For William Carlos Williams

as the T'ang poet said
    the scene
            of a poem
                    is like the smoke
    that issues from
        fine jade
            when the sun
                    is warm

you
    have the touch
            that makes the poet's line
                    come true

but who
    can learn
        this difficult
                art
and who
    but a few
        can see the smoke
            of fine jade?

Harold Norse

EXTRACT FROM THE "JAGUARS"

The Jaguars are coming. Yes. They are
coming closing in on all sides. It is high
time for the Jaguars to arrive. The are all
coming tomorrow. Very early in the morning
before breakfast. Not just a few but many.
Perhaps even thousands if not hundreds of
thousands. They are coming for sure. That's
what they said when they said they were coming. Tomorrow at three o'clock to be more
precise. The Jaguars.

Norman Bluhm

60

HAROLD NORSE

NANOS VALAORITIS

BOB KAUFMAN

FROM NOW ON
PRESIDENTS'
HAVE TO BE
MOVIE STARS.
Bob Kaufman

KIRBY DOYLE

JOHN MUELLER

Lithe this morning
    drinking beer
in a waterfront bar
I realize that
poetry is finer
& more living
than life itself,
& take the option
to celebrate
that we lived
    by poetry,
to celebrate
that
we lived poetry.

Kirby Doyle

No USE FOR LIGHTNING MIND. IT IS A SLOW ENFOLDING

THAT I GET TO KNOW

ALICE NOTLEY

DAVID HENDERSON

66

COMPLINE

The Earth is one word deep
that is your name.

Alice Notley
10/7/85

SANTO STATION
beTween WORLds
VORTex oF MeRcy
border oF hope
deiFicaTion of desiRe
CombusTion of FeAR
MAsTeRy beloved

D. J. Henderson
Fr. SANTO STATION written
in Boulder Colo June 1981

ED SANDERS

RICHARD BRAUTIGAN

68

The restitution
        of the oculus
is the foundation
        of theology

Ed Sanders

June 1985

This photograph was taken in May.
I gave the hat away in November,
so you'll never see me wearing it again.

Richard Brautigan

LAWRENCE DURRELL

Its fatal to love

Lawrence Durrell
(Pursewarden)

AMIRI BARAKA

JESSICA HAGEDORN

Change is the only Constant
Revolution the only
Solution !

Amiri Baraka 1984

a Song of Bullets   (- for Paloma)

War is predicted
in five years, ten years
any day now
I always thought
it was already happening

snipers & poets locked
in a secret embrace
the country my child
may never see

a heritage of women
in heat
and men skilled
at betrayal
dancing
to the song of bullets.

Jessica Hagedorn

CAROLYN FORCHÉ

ERNESTO CARDENAL

The Visitor

In Spanish he whispers there is no time left.
It is the sound of scythes arcing in wheat,
the ache of some field song in Salvador.
The wind along the prison, cautious
as Francisco's hands on the inside, touching
the walls as he walks, it is his wife's breath
slipping into his cell each night while he
imagines his hand to be hers. It is a small country.

There is nothing one man will not do to another.

Carolyn Forché, 1979
San Salvador

transcribed 1985 New York

La revolución no es ilusión.

Ernesto Cardenal

Solentiname. Febrero 2, 84.

ROBERTO VARGAS

FERNANDO ALEGRIA

Who ASKS - IN A JUNGLE ?

do I/WE MISS your kissing / slightly witheld
From ME/US ALWAYS LEAVING your Womaneeds
and our children IN "Barrios" where kisses
sometimes pretend TruTh and other HANDS
Hold yours INSTEAD of Their "COMBATIVE SHARE"
OF The condition OF Being Poor young and
3RD WORLD) MUSICAL Finger where reach out TO PLAY
you [HONK&H] DRIVEN TRUCK SURE IN
SOME DREAM for A MOMENT...FAMILIAR/DISTANT
AGAINST THE ASPHALT SONG TURNED Revolution
LEAVING you AGAINST The rythm of OUR
KISSING SLIGHTLY ShoT OUT FROM IN
FRONT OF US while IN TROPIC HOMELAND RIFLED
HANDS HOLDING Their Share of OUR CONDITION
OF Being Poor grown y NICARAGUAN SALVADORLANS
AFRICANOS STILL IN NEED OF YOUR KISSING
SLIGHTLY AS I/WE LEAVE you 1 hundred TIMES
TO POTENTIAL Bedroom Commandos GROWN FAT
WITH KISSES AND I/wE TURN BONE
WITHOUT
THEM

Guerrilla Phase I
FOR WOMEN LEFT
BEHIND —   Roberto '76

" ... de los desaparecidos es el reino
de la tierra."
  "... De los justos el reino del
cielo. "

Jesus Olguin

In sound and sense it is the music of inner relationships that moves me

ROBERT DUNCAN

THULANI DAVIS

MICHAEL PALMER

black spaces

for Robert Hayden

in the black and few spaces
i find my five
to make my own
meet the marauders
where they live & die
in the black & few spaces
where human recall comes strong
like bars of peace be still
their prophets are common folks
who live among neighbors
and eat friendly bread
in the black & few spaces
where i can listen to you
we all have lovers
bodies leave impressions
yes, there are still sacred spaces
dance moving through them . . . .

Thulani Davis

(Baudelaire series)

You, island in this page
image in this page

what if things really did
correspond, silk to breath

evening to eyelid
bread to thread

Michael Palmer

81

ROBERT CREELEY

SAD ADVICE

If it isn't fun, don't do it.
You'll have enough to do that isn't.

Such is life, like they say,
no one gets away without paying

and since you don't get to keep it
anyhow, who needs it.

Robert Rimler

CLAYTON ESHLEMAN

CHRISTOPHER ISHERWOOD

UN POCO LOCO

Bird Powell's story is never complete.
The image of a man playing blues
Who earlier that day

sipped lunch on all fours
is rudimentary turning, crawling
chorus after chorus, lifting I Covers,

to view simmering Waterfront splinters,
he is visiting fist shacks,
the sipped milk becomes a dug root,

he bites into the horizon
wearing Keyboard braces, he winds within
the steel cord all

who have pulled through mother recall
as the bastard spirit beyond her strength.

~ Clayton Eshleman
L.A.   1980

With my best wishes,

Christopher Isherwood.

January 19 1985

Santa Monica

ABHORRENCES
Boulder, Oct/1985

Something we can all agree on
_____

Suppose there were a new
acronym for an old disease—
very awful & very incurable.
Let's call it HELPS for

Heritable Endemic Longrange
Poverty Syndrome
Now here's the Question:
Do you think there would be
much tea & sympathy for this plague?
Neither do I.

Gregory Corso

ED DORN

MICHAEL BROWNSTEIN

JAYNE CORTEZ

I may be quite childish
to insist on eating
breathless stars of a winter sky
discovered in her glance
muscular herald appears next
spireas with misty white and pink plumes
seeds of winter cherry, seeds of blue lupin
the pump wrapped in straw
her nose against the root of her tail
Mouth quivering as it waits

—Michael Brownstein

Some-
Times
I
feel
like
a
Roaring
Black
Jaguar
Pacing
through
the
Cage
of
a
Paris
Zoo

11/6/85

And it is a dream sailing in a
dark unprotected cove
("37 Haiku)

John Ashbery

JOHN ASHBERY

DRUMMOND HADLEY

BILL BERKSON

"a leg each side of a horse's back,
a mind in the middle...."

Drum Hadley

Can you explain yourself to this life?
It's a small desert. You see a faint
figure on the horizon — vaguely disheveled,
bottle in mouth, waving a shirt — probably
your friend.

for Chris Felver
A Se Stesso

Bill Berkson
Sept. 1981.

West Wall

In the unmade light I can see the world
as the leaves brighten I see the air
the shadows melt and the apricots appear
now that the branches vanish I see the apricots
from a thousand trees ripening in the air
they are ripening in the sun along the west wall
apricots beyond number are ripening in the daylight

Whatever was there
I never saw those apricots swaying in the light
I might have stood in orchards forever
without beholding the day in the apricots
or knowing the ripeness of the lucid air
or vouching the apricots in your skin
or tasting in your mouth the sun in the apricots

W S Merwin

W. S. MERWIN

JOHN LOGAN

EUGENE RUGGLES

96

On a photograph by Aaron Siskind

Ghost of the Master's hand!
Glove of Aaron Siskind! I
feel your canvas touch
flicked with lead spots of paint
upon the cold point of my heart.
    18 June '85   John Logan

Inscription for the Door

I have no enemies left,
only some friends who are late.
Come in, there is no lock, hang your coat
beside the fire and pull a chair to its edge.
We shall drink new tea, then clean the path
leading back to the hearts first address.
You may have news of these nations beginning
to revolve beside each other like seasons
or word of the fires out of control south of us,
where the poor are burning the lies keeping them poor...

                    —Eugene Ruggles
                    6-20-85

STANLEY KUNITZ

I can scarcely wait till tomorrow
when a new life begins for me,
as it does each day,
as it does each day.

Stanley Kunitz

KENWARD ELMSLIE

JOHN GODFREY

POEM FOR DOC
FROM THE GOOD OLD DAYS

I love U
I love U so mucho
I love U so mucho mucho
I love U so mucho mucho mucho

I'm bestride myself
On a whizzy carousel
U between my thighs
All the way to hell

but be patient
make up takes time
in the Tunnel of Love

polish up the mirrors OK hon?
I love U so mucho mucho mucho
I love U so mucho mucho
I love U so mucho

even in funhouse mirrors
I love U

Kenward Elmslie
Nov 13, 1985

Vultures know I am not dead to rights
I dress as an officer at night
I wear the gray city perfume
that is as garlic to a martyr's sniff
while in vain punks kiss at my heels
(from "What It Takes")
John Godfrey

101

This is &
and I am &
and you are &
and so is that
and he is &
and she is &
and it is &
and that is that

James Broughton

JAMES BROUGHTON

JACK HIRSCHMAN

ISHMAEL REED

You are NOT a slave
and I am NOT a machine
and This is NOT
an opium dream,
Comrade.

Jack Hirschman

Nov 30 1981
Dear Chris Felver,

Nobody is ever photographed
my face quite this way.
I don't know whether
to mount the face or send it to
the National Space Administration;
It looks like something somebody
ought to launch; not wear.

Best,
Jack Micheline

105

VICTOR HERNANDEZ CRUZ

BERNADETTE MAYER

On the street
never associate one thing with what you see
standing next to it—
Always walk around the corner—

— victor hernández cruz —
nueva york 1/86—

No Nukes

Then the fat ape is a car care nonnuclear
It's ten even here over the mushroom cloud
It's a bite alot, go to it military men!
Horn tool baby look oil! Be greedy!
Out up use fun maybe or cluster bombs
Get joy yet but how?
China + she he thin + then, gone
Leisure rings for a go no bombs then

Bernadette Mayer

Art is as old in America as it is in Europe, if not older —

The dead dinosaur, our unfortunate relation, is not bewailed. We do however bewail the living whale (greenpeace etc) — Thus we are living artists in art in America. consider this — I speak of LIFE IN ART... help preserve it... or else it'll become oil; the polluting spirit of dinosaur. S Corso

To BE is to Do (DESCANTES)

To Do is to BE (SARTRE)

DO BE DO BE DO (SINATRA

Contribes by

Gregory Corso

GREGORY CORSO

TED JOANS

HOWARD HART

The Truth

If you should see
a man
Walking down
a crowded street
talking a L o u d
to himself
Don't Run
In the opposite direction
But run toward him
For he is a poet!
You have nothing to fear
from the poet
but
   the
   Truth

Poetry is rhythm and music within words and thought; the ability to not say no when the answer is yes, to beauty.

Howard Hart

MICHAEL McCLURE

THE EVOLUTION OF MICROBES,
THE PATTERNS OF THE MANOUVERS
OF GNATS —These things
increase us - but bring no
surcease to our hunger
for the soft fleshiness
of experience. I long power
and black knowledge
FREED
of constraint
but to touch them
without knowing
the petals
of tulips of marigolds
leaves me with complaint

I MUST SEE AGAIN

BE BRIGHT

AND
HOWL!
Michael McClure

EILEEN MYLES

JIM CARROL

114

In a world
where champagne
is more
accessible
than water

you can't
sell poems
about
thirst.   (From
                   "Without
                   Art")

                Eileen
                Myles

Note for Song
         (the)
On my minor she wrote,
           "Vaya con Dio"
Next to my photo of
           Delores del Rio

                Jim Carroll
                     '85

115

Old Woman Nature

naturally has a bag of bones
        tucked away somewhere.
        a whole roomfull of bones!
a scattering of hair and cartilage
bits in the woods.
A fox scat with hair and a tooth
                in it.
        a shellmound
            a bone flake in a streambank.

A purring cat, crunching
the mouse head first
        eating on down toward the tail —
the sweet old woman
calmly gathering firewood
            in the moon —
Don't be shocked,
She's heating you some soup!

on seeing _Kurozuka_ at the Tokyo Kabuki-za VII : 81

                Gary Snyder

GARY SNYDER

116

MAUREEN OWEN

LARRY EIGNER

Calcium

Of course I got up & went out
to try to talk to you   about the immediate

Casual boards rocked — the phosphorous skies
+ creaked fantastically
I thought about my bones
I love my bones
Sometimes I rest my chin on
my knee
+ my lips brush the skin

its   an awkward position

Maureen
Owen

Oct — New York

TIME SEEMS MY-
STERIOUS
ESPECIALLY
AFTER DARK

NOW IS THAT THE
UNIVERSE

CALM
WIDNER

(BLIND
IN ORBIT)

"Time seems mysterious especially after dark
now is that the universe"

119

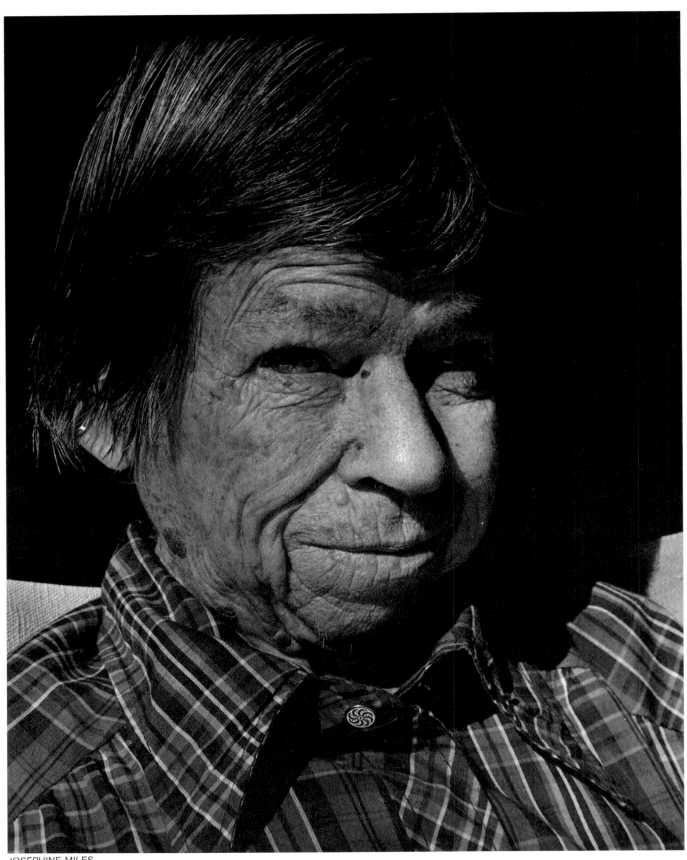

JOSEPHINE MILES

140 Wilson Wy
Saratoga 94939

a statement in form of a photograph
from Saratoga — Chris Felver
from Jo Mills
March 1982

LARRY FAGIN

MARY FERRARI

I was young but not in my
heart
as I came to consciousness
of the world

[signature]

Virgil prefers trees
So do I
Yet lean back
deferring necessarily
to Aeneas at sea.
(from "Agenda")
Mary Ferrari

123

Radiant Opal

The languorous undle
Through the thicket
The humming glen
Sights
The raven of the rainbow

Philip Lamantia

PHILIP LAMANTIA

BARBARA GUEST

ANSELM HOLLO

126

Later... while he arranged his camera, admiring
as always his adroitness, the rapidity with which
his preparations took place as just before the
shutter fell his lens sheltered her face.

"The Countess from Minneapolis"

Barbara Guest

SOMETHING I STOLE,
& WOULD LIKE YOU TO SEE

EROS
totally involved love at first sight

LUDUS
playful love -- love as a game

STORGE
love from a deep and lasting friendship

PRAGMA
love with a shopping list

MANIA
unbalanced love involving extreme possessiveness

AGAPE
selfless love making no demand for love in return

PARADISO
all of the above in perfect perennially contradictory balance

Anselm Hollo

THUS DID I, PONDERING OUR
MYRIAD INSCRUTABLE DESTINIES
HIDDEN IN TIME.....

Lawrence Ferlinghetti

at City Lights 6/81

LAWRENCE FERLINGHETTI

LEWIS WARSH

NANCY JOYCE PETERS

SELF - PORTRAIT

As if in myself there was
a feeling of timidity I could
sense was part of me, + say
To myself, That's what I'm like ...

LWANSA

---

a couple of lines from The Western Wars

Bare-knuckled — poetry subsides on the
tender breast of silkstockinged day
& pennants all colors kiss the breezes of
nepenthe under the mask of intellect —
Just as the stalk of rubies is growing
from the forehead of the Absolute,
I know it is raining in the futile heart
illimitable as the prairie

Nancy Joyce Peters

JOHN CAGE

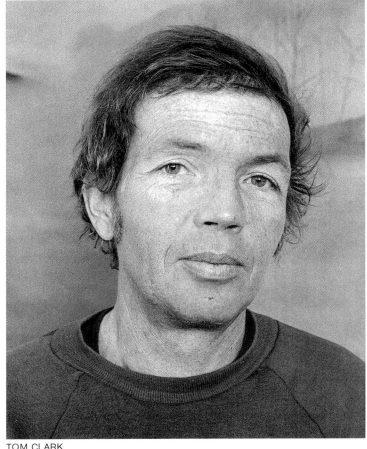

TOM CLARK

take as challenge project earth
to make it virgin
as it used to be
but with technology (cake and eat it too)

John Cage Oct. '85

May 11, 1985:
for Chris
Felver

Teflon and Velcro
_____

To get ahead
in this world of ours
you've got to have
a hide as tough
& a head as hard
as Teflon
and in addition
you've got to know
how to hook into
the powers that be
as perfectly
as though they and you
were matching slabs
of Velcro

Tom Clark

133

Since dreams are a biologic
necessity we are literally
'such stuff as dreams are
made of' and real poetry is dream.

William S. Burroughs

WILLIAM BURROUGHS

NO VISITORS.

BUKOWSKI

EPILOGUE

Much of this work came to exist through a very spontaneous and unstructured process, a very life-like process, one poet putting me in touch with another poet, over the phone, over a meal, starting in San Francisco and the Santa Cruz Mountains, through Boulder, to New York City, back and forth over America. For me the most rewarding and nourishing aspect of this experience was the natural pattern that kept unfolding. It opened me.

Originally, I was very moved by Man Ray's collection of European poets from the surrealist period. I grew to feel America must be as rich with its own gift of poets. The enormous cross-section of lives I encountered has sustained this feeling for me; they have kept me moving, long after the last photograph was opening before me.

Last night while making the final prints for this book, a passage from Apollinaire quite literally fell into my hands, a passage that instantly became a culmination, a kind of framing I would like to leave this book with.

"There are poets to whom a muse dictates their works, there are artists whose hand is guided by an unknown being who uses them like an instrument. There is no such thing for them as fatigue for they do not work, although they can produce a great deal at any time, on any day, in any country, in all seasons; they are not men but poetic or artistic instruments."

Chris Felver
San Francisco
February 1986

AFTERWORD

A Letter to Chris Felver

Dear Chris:

Good friend, where will you be next? To what next face or place will you and your camera respond? You, if not in Europe, Miami, or Mexico City, then in Sun Valley; catching the spiritual air at Naropa in Boulder; on mission for Ferlinghetti and yourself with Cardenal in Nicaragua, or shooting and trucking in North Beach or Bolinas above San Francisco. One day in L.A., seemingly thirty minutes later in Maine, then Manhattan. Come now, Chris, I telephoned you in Vermont on a Wednesday, and then, but a few days later, a mailgram arrived from you in China, telling me about your visit to the Beijing Opera. I once told a mutual friend that if I, alone, were to stand once more next to that Coke machine atop Milan Cathedral, the only person I would expect to come strutting out from behind one of those multitudinous crocketed pinnacles, camera clicking or videopack humming, would be Chris Felver. In his commentary in *French Primitive Photography* (1969) Robert Sobieszek tells us that, in 1858, Victor Fournel said:

> ...It is not given to everybody to be able to amble naively, that man is a mobile and empassioned daguerreotype who secures the most subtle traces, and in whom is reproduced, with their changing reflections, the march of things, the movement of the city, the multiple physiognomy of the public spirit, beliefs, antipathies and admirations of the crowd.

Did you impress Fornel in a former life? Does he see you at work from some spiritual plateau? Still fitting well the shoes of Fournel's ambling man, you are a remarkable *flâneur*—as even Baudelaire, despite his contempt for photography, would have likely identified your peripatetical being, your observations, your camerawork: Everywhere! Here, you have brought us silver presences of many poets *now*, their faces, autographic names, and fragments of writing defined especially for *The Poet Exposed*. Again, as is always the case in your photographic work, you have generously and admirably honored the "creative others," those well and little known. You, again, prove to be the most selfless visual chronicler of significant selves today. That is the major feature of your style, and many love you for exactly that! And I thank you for asking me to offer an afterword to this wonderful gallery of poets. There is too much to say about a book so good and I don't want to offer any academic afterthoughts, but perhaps "selfishly" in the face of your "selflessness," to share something about my love for photography and poetry, and to reflect on some of the reasons why I find your photographs of the poets and their own scripted signals of consciousness about self, about face, about poetry, so moving and so touching, so indicative that there is still hope for all of us as long as the poet can be present amongst us to sing.

Although many times reconfigured in those lineup snaps for the family album, I remember well my first real encounter with the photographic, in Neptune Beach, Florida, right below the Georgia line. Brother Dan and I, he in the fourth grade and I in the third, as usual needed money, particularly when Mama and sisters Clara Jean and Thelma Ann were away to Jacksonville in the old black Packard, leaving us to "be good Sunday-school boys" and to watch over our old garage-apartment. That day, the day the sun produced a miracle, remains vividly present in my mind. We prepared a guaranteed money-making extravaganza right in the combined living/dining room: throw rugs turned into tents over the sparse furniture; my tempera-painted scenes of Hawaii copied from *National Geographic*, and the best faces of Dick Tracy and Popeye, on Piggly Wiggly grocery bags tacked to pine walls; Dan's volcano—dry ice from the icebox dumped into a soda-water filled washtub surmounted by a huge newspaper cone—belched noxious fog. And for the major attraction, a sliding board, down the never-used, enclosed front stairs, a slide made from mildewed E-Z Curve paperboard left from one of the projects Daddy never got to, a slide that turned away from the rusted-shut door at the bottom of the stairwell into an old adjoining shower stall in the garage. From the upper landing of the back-door steps, we trumpeted kids-coded invitational signals on hollowed-out cowhorns plucked from the parched skulls of lightning-struck cattle discovered on one of our many secret ventures to the town dump. Our gang came, and, democratically, for any coin, they were admitted to our room of delights. Having ignored the murals,

danced around the volcano, destroyed the tents, they were ushered to the slide. At least seven had descended before the ominous sound of that Packard cut the air. I, to escape the force of an angry trio of womenkin come home too soon, jumped for the slide. Down there below, like an upside down grape-cluster, were the heads of those seven, viewing an inverted and laterally reversed tiny scene cast on that inclined stairwell slide: Varnetta Croy, she who always stole our early fascination, hanging up laundry outside her shack, against a backdrop of sand dunes and the waves of the Atlantic ocean. Coming through the keyhole of that permanently closed door into that darkened stairwell, that never-suspected camera obscura, were the moving traces of Varnetta, her glistening arms and legs, her flapping slips and bloomers, blowing sand and white-lipped swells, kinetically, synchronistically, dimly focused upon that sliding board; projected, as I would later learn, by the "pencil of nature," by the actinic rays of the Florida sun reflecting off and carrying Varnetta and her secret things right into our as yet unripe laps. Such fixating wonder allowed for no escape; those imaging beams of light a sufficient trade-off for the smacking wrath of, first, hands and broom, and later, belt. Our fannies were blistered, but no matter! From that point on I was hooked on photography! And for no other more important reason, that is why I, like you, photograph constantly, and why I for twenty-seven years have taught the history of photography, a history, need I remind, originating in the Paleolithic caves despite that some fools still naively believe the wonders of the medium began in 1839.

And poetry? But suggestions! The black man who guided the glass-bottom boat at Silver Springs seemed like a real poet to me, chanting over and over again, as we looked down into the crystalline water, *See the fishes touch their noses, see the ferns as they grow-ses; dip you han into the water, keep your seat where you oughter,* his melliloquent baritone commands mesmerizing my soul. And Reverend Stout's reading of the Psalms with no spaces between the words: how well I remember the machine-gun rhythms of those still cryptic Psalmic "prayers for help, and against enemies" shouted from his pulpit, when I was thirteen during World War II. Goodman Stout's *Moab/is/my/washpot/ over/Edom/will/I/cast/my/shoe/over/Philistia/will/ I/triumph* remains my ridiculously magic hedge against foes. My favorite book, then: Louis Untermeyer's 1945 edition of *Pocket Book of Story Poems*, purloined from the school library where it was placed under the sign RESTRICTED. It was in that little book, its acid-cracked pages retained to this day, I discovered John Davidson's late-nineteenth-century recast of the legendary "Ballad of a Nun": she,... *fittest bride/Of Christ in all the diocese*; she, who, before her final reclamation by the Virgin Mary, longed to ...*use her blood*, to ...*taste of love at last!*, who ...*doffed her outer robe,/And sent it sailing down the blast*; she who *Half-naked through the town...went*; and gave ...*a grave youth nobly dressed;/...all her passion's hoard*; to become *The strangest woman ever seen./...a mermaiden./...a ghoul,.../A heathen goddess born again./...a she-wolf, gaunt and grim!* No wonder that RESTRICTED sign! Living in that downward slope of the Bible Belt where even dancing was a sin, that ballad, that Nun, not her light but her shadow, her mysterious wants, blooded in me a downright gluttonous appetite for anecdotal poetry. Somehow, like Huck, I thought going to hell on poetry was the perfect antidote for my every Sunday off-key suffering and pinchface angelicism as a forced member of the junior high choir at the Golgotha Presbyterian Church. In *Story Poems*, I first learned never to serve war on reading Tennyson's lines: *Not tho' the soldier knew/Some one had blunder'd:/Theirs not to make reply,/Theirs not to reason why,/Theirs but to do and die.* Maybe that's why the poetic voices of Ginsberg and Bly seemed so right later on. And why Jessica Hagedorn's "The Song of Bullets" and Bernadette Mayer's "No Nukes," inscribed here in *The Poet Exposed*, seem so right today. In *Story Poems*, I discovered Service's ...*the lady that's known as Lou*; read verse about those wondrous characters: Roy Bean, Sam Bass, Parson Gray, Juggling Jerry, Jim Bludso, John Barleycorn; about what I would later know to name Oedipal desire and transvestism in the tale of "Childe Maurice"; about how *Kind hearts are more than coronets* from an encounter with "Lady Clara Vere de Vere"; about, though then only incipiently understanding, cruel egotism and hateful pride in that miracle of condensation—a novel in fifty-six lines—"My Last Duchess," by Browning. And more! Other books, other poems! What adolescent could have found a more provocative fueling of lust than those lines from Charlotte Mew's "The Farmer's Bride:" ...*Oh! my God! the down,/The soft young down of her, the brown,/The brown of her—her eyes, her hair, her hair!*? Eventually, Frank Doggett—my high-school principal, avid fisherman, ribald humorist, a scholar of now international renown still devoting his life to the study and explication of poetry, particularly the works of Wallace Stevens—found the first large audience for his extraordinary critical consciousness in senior schoolchildren eager to hear his analyses of Donne, Lovelace, Marvell, Keats, Blake, Hardy, Whitman, Baudelaire, Rimbaud, Mallarmé. What other twelfth-grader in 1950 America was so privileged to learn, as we did from Doggett, of the "singing bird" motif in poetry past and present; the nature of concrete poetry relative to cubist painting; how the poet Jules Laforgue, later Elizabethan dramatists, even a Jamesian

atmosphere, informed the work of T. S. Eliot? How I would sit upon the shores of Neptune Beach and worry about becoming like Prufrock, *To wonder, "Do I dare?" and, "Do I dare?"/...Do I dare/Disturb the universe?*, while, from the Atlantic, I also had

> ...heard the mermaids singing, each to each./...seen them riding seaward on the waves/ Combing the white hair of the waves blown back/When the wind blows the water white and black./...Till human voices wake us, and we drown.

Notwithstanding but primitive achievement in math and science, a paper I wrote on "The Love Song of J. Alfred Prufrock" and John Donne's "Song" (*Go and catch a falling star*), and Doggett's help, won me a scholarship at Kenyon College. From John Crowe Ransom, I would learn to

> ...dip my hat to Chaucer,/Swilling soup from his saucer,/And to Master Shakespeare/Who wrote big on small beer./.../Sing a song for Percy Shelley, Drowned in pale lemon jelly,/And for precious John Keats,/Dripping blood of pickled beets.

Alas, that "Survey of Literature" was beyond my purse, and I pursued studies in art and photography at the University of Florida. Nevertheless, between pictures, I was swilling at the trough of the sacred with Milton as guide, learning from Dylan Thomas what it's like *When only the moon rages/ And the lovers lie abed/With all their griefs in their arms*; from Wallace Stevens more reasons to remain obsessed with *Lol-lolling the endlessness of poetry*.

Having now come close to the age of that ...*sixty-year-old smiling public man* in Yeats's "Among School Children," I know how poetry has guided my life. Above all, I know how Rilke's poems and his *Letters to a Young Poet* cannot escape my continuous dependency:

> If you will cling to Nature, as the simple in Nature, to the little things that hardly any one sees, and that can so unexpectedly become big and beyond measuring; if you have this love of inconsiderable things and seek quite humbly as a ministrant to win the confidence of what seems poor: then everything will become easier, more coherent and somehow more conciliatory for you, not in your intellect, perhaps, which lags behind astonished, but in your inmost consciousness, waking and cognizance...try to love *the questions themselves* like locked rooms and like books that are written in a very foreign tongue...live everything. *Live* the questions now. Perhaps you will then gradually, without noticing it, live along some distant day into the answer...take to yourself whatever comes with great trust, and if only it comes out of your own will, out of some need of your inmost being, take it upon yourself and hate nothing.

Oh, fore and aft midlife crisis, how Sylvia Plath's "Daddy" horrified my heart; cultivated my imagination in evil; made me know the shadow side of being! When I became too rational, how Philip Lamantia brought me back to feeling again, to revalue the oneiric exoticism found in the psychic domain of the "uroboric," that mind state wherein there is a universal overlappingness of all things and beings, wherein *The burning manes of the midnight jungle/announce sleep coming on the fatal horses/of love/an explosive pearl in the sea-shell of sleep* (From "Invisible" in *Touch of the Marvelous*, 1974). How W. S. Merwin's poems relieved my sometimes loneliness, offering the keys to an unconditional life: *something needs me/everything needs me/I need myself/and the fire is my father* (From "A Flea's Carrying Words" in *Writings to an Unfinished Accompaniment*, 1976). How Michael McClure—who, here in *The Poet Exposed*, reminds that *I MUST SEE AGAIN/BE BRIGHT/AND/ HOWL!*—enabled me, in his *Ghost Tantras* (1969), to roar poetry, without embarrassment, like a beast discovering song:

THRAHHR THONETT GRAHH
ROO-OOOOOOOO-OOOOOOOOO-OOOOOR!
Place wings upon words and rohrs.
Grahhgrool gahrooo wipps mahoove.
OOH NOH THOW MEE TOH TORNY
seeking
eternity
THOU-ME
THOW!
!GAHROOOOOOOOOOH!.

How grateful I am to Naomi Lazard and Carolyn Kizer for bringing to my life the simple, sincere, sensuous, courageous songs of the Urdu poet Faiz Ahmed Faiz, a poetry of peace and social concern, a poetry of, as Lazard has defined it, "almost unutterable sweetness, a melting of sweetness that has nothing to do with sentimentality and is a million miles away from being saccharine" (From *Translating Faiz Ahmed Faiz: A Memoir and a Memoriam*, Columbia, 1984). Enough! Obviously, Chris, these few suggestions tell you I am an unbridled dilettante when it comes to poetry. Of that I am proud, for, as Heinrich Zimmer wrote in *The King and the Corpse* (1948):

> The dilettante—Italian *dilettante* (present participle of the verb *dilettare*, "to take delight in"—is one who takes delight (*diletto*) in something. . . . What characterizes the dilettante is his delight in the always preliminary nature of his never-to-be-culminated understanding.

My romance with poetry is a primary delight! Soon, on one of many shelves in every room of home— my, my wife's, and my poet daughter's home— alongside a hundred-plus titles affirming poetry as necessary to life, shall rest *The Poet Exposed*, offering new lodes to mine. What can but hint of its powerful messagings for both photography and poetry?

Paul Valéry wrote, in "On Portraits" (1928), that "The human face is the most individual of all things..." and that "we are absolutely compelled, from childhood, to learn to read the human countenance... the face as we see it presents, as it were, a series of possibilities." Ishmael Reed, in *The Poet Exposed*, writes to you, Chris, of the surprising evidence and potentialities of his face as you have arrested its presence through a contract between his light and your lens: "Nobody's ever photographed my face quite this way. I don't know whether to mount the face or send it to the National Space Administration; it looks like something somebody ought to land on, not wear." Not only does the proximity of your hand-held Nikon, but your own consistent closeness to the poets, typically eighteen to twenty inches between you, your camera and them, brings me to sense, as if, I could touch the physiognomies; that such proximity to their faces might tempt radical visitations: I love landing on Reed's inquisitive eyes, on Bobbie Louise Hawkins' luminous teeth, lunar guests in her gorgeous smile *caught out of the void, caught onto paper*. I want to curl up in Everson's mane; kiss the courage and the tenderness of Cardenal's smile; climb the sunlit peaks, rest in the dark furrows, glide through the prairies of the archetypally earthly visage of Josephine Miles; leap from those oriental calligraphs, onto the track of that linear nimbus which leads my eye to eavesdrop on what's behind Gary Snyder's brow. What facial sites; what occasions for sight! Many of your portraits remind me of Kenneth Patchen's lines: *There is no betrayal in the human face./Time's fin, hoof, wing, and fang struggle there* (From "To Whom It May Concern," 1939). Many prompt me to reconsider that fragment from *Macbeth*: *...face...is a book where men/May read strange matters*. Many of these instantaneously mirrored portraits make me find in them what Walt Whitman found: *In the faces of men and women I see God,/and in my/own face in the glass,/I find letters from God dropt in the street, and every/one signed in God's name*. Some seem like fellow animals in whose reappearance now as past-tense images we are made to search their eyes, noses, mouths, cheeks, to discover some missing link to ourselves, realizing, as John Logan has written, *We want to find a kind of King Kong/(magnificent but wrong)/caught and salted safe as us/behind the bars of flesh,/behind the glass of the face* (From "The Zoo," 1963). And if we think we shall finally know these faces of poets, memorizing their presences refigured on these tablets of black and white, a deeper stare into the atomistic grains of silver that coalesce *to make a face*, or the someday good fortune to see *face to face* in fact, will make us know, as Faiz's lines still breathe: *How the features, learned by heart, of a single face,/alter at once, and bloom before your eyes* (From "If I Were Certain," translated by Carolyn Kizer, in *Excerpts from a Pakistan Journal*, 1969). We may evade the originally animate, the once upon a moment, split-second actuality of any one of these outward aspects, affirming Philip Whalen's note about his portrait that *This printed face doesn't see/a curious world looking in—/Big map of nothing.* Yet, despite the silencing of voice in a photographic print, we can imagine, with John Berger's *And our faces, my heart, brief as photos* (1984) as the right chart for a proleptic reengagement of these poets' stilled being, that:

> The face looks straight at me and without words, by the expression of the eyes alone, it affirms the reality of its existence. As if my gaze had called out a name, and the face, by returning it, was answering, "Present!"

Jack Micheline states for you, Chris, that *The role of the artist is to raise the light* and your photographic portraits of these poets have done that raising well. When I see your work, I am glad I don't feel inclined to say, "I see there a Felver," as I am often bound to name the photographer first and then the subject viewed when encountering the work of impressive picture makers, such as, say, Strand, Weston, Avedon. I sense that the *en face* directness of your work proves you might question the morality of a surreptitiously captured portrait such as Strand's famous "Blind Woman, New York" (1916), achieved secretly by his attachment of a false lens to the side of his Ensign reflex; that bogus lens aimed away from the woman, as if he were attentive to other things, while the real lens of the camera, under his left arm, partly concealed by his sleeve, committed what Ben Maddow identifies as its "90° deception:" (*FACES*, 1977), a right-angle ruse to gain a masterpiece while she knew not her face, her light, was being so poignantly, so viciously trapped. When we read Edward Weston's *Random Notes on Photography* (1922), wherein he says that "Only the photographer can register ... all the many vital instants of life which 'affirm the majesty of the moment,'" how often do we witness in his magnificent portraits, not the subject's moment but Weston's own abstracting strategies, his intentionalist mask more timely than the photographed persona? And when overcome, astonished, by Avedon's brobdingnagian, strobe-chiseled faces inevitably decon textualized as they loom from the white Sahara of their seamless grounds, do we seriously consider his own recorded words, "Sometimes I think all my pictures are just pictures of me"? If, as Ed Sanders states, *The restitution of the oculus is the foundation of theology*, and if a contemporary photographical theology could be defined to offer pictorial assertions about letting faces be what they are, not what a photographer wants them to be, your faces of these poets should serve as a fine testament; not only echoing the old time religion of daguerreotypes, calotypes, ambrotypes, *cartes-de-visite*, and cabinet images wherein face, not style, was reverenced, but also revealing a splendid new chapter in photographic candor whereby portraits excellently achieved are free of formal prejudice and stylistic disguise. David Meltzer's penned pictographic notation of the little face in the box, that face seemingly defined, as I see it, by the dash-line particles of light emanating from a sizzling pinwheel floret-sun, precisely what *The Poet Exposed* achieves: Chris, the power of your vision, your smile, your camera BRINGS THE FACE OF MUSIC BACK, ATOM BY ATOM. Equally, Barbara Guest reveals what you have constructed with light and atomistic silver: *while he arranged his camera, admiring as always his adroitness, the rapidity with which his preparations took place as just before the shutter fell his lens sheltered her face.* For me your adept photography has given these poets not only splendid presence but touching *shelter*. And finally, your photographs in *The Poet Exposed* richly reveal to my vision what Ted Joans has writ with such verve for me to ever sing, as if both of you were defining again what I have always known: *You have nothing to fear from the poet but the Truth.*

Handshake, Chris. Keep Shining!

William E. Parker
Professor of Art & History of Photography
Department of Art, School of Fine Arts
The University of Connecticut (Storrs)

POETS INDEX